PLANET AVOIDANCE

By Anne-Marie Barton

& ILLUSTRATED BY HARRY P.W.

What is compliance?

Doing as you are told or instructed, is compliance.

What is avoidance?

Avoiding doing as you are told or instructed, is avoidance.

The word crime here means you have found a 'tool' to help you cope with a demand, and still feel safe. This is called a demand compliance tool (crime). It is called a 'crime' as many here must avoid demands, instead of coping with them. It is how we all feel safe on our planet.

Most people on our planet feel safe if they do not comply with any demands...

But there are a small few who feel safe by giving in and complying to demands.

I have heard that on planet Earth the opposite is true. Most people on your planet give in to demands. There are some very talented people on Earth who have to avoid demands to feel safe.

On Earth it is not a crime whichever way you feel safe. It sounds like a lovely planet!

Demands are everywhere,

on planet Avoidance it

gives us quite a scare!

What are demands?

If you are told what to do or given a set of instructions, these can be demands!

Demands:

A timetable

Leaving the house

Getting dressed

Staying clean

Doing something well

Being asked questions

Eating when hungry

Needing the toilet

Wanting to do something

Needing to sleep

Reading a book

The list goes on and on…

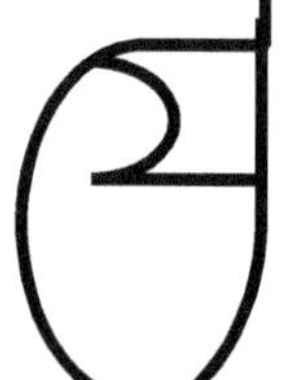

There is such a long list of demands for everyone, every day. Even when you really enjoy and want to do something... that is a demand too!

It does all sound very confusing, doesn't it?

But it is ok… we all need to understand our

differences, as we all are unique.

Isn't that a strange word? – unique!

It means we are all different, and that it is

good to be different.

So, here on planet Avoidance we like to be free of

demands. We enjoy doing things our own way. Our

brains decide when to do something and our brains do

not like the bossy demands!

Let me explain by telling you

one of my solved compliance

crimes...

Last year, a boy from our planet

was told by his teacher that he

must learn the alphabet. This was a

demand, but he did as he was told

(he complied).

As I had heard him singing his ABCs and

other people talking of his compliance, I

had to arrest him. (Do not worry, here it

does not mean the same thing as it does on

planet Earth.)

You see even though it is a 'crime', he

did very well to cope with complying

to this demand.

He had to be taken to the recovery jail (a

magical place for recovery). It is a place of

your own imagination and it helps you to

recover by using your tools.

Here anyone who

complies to a demand

is given time to

recover and rest. It is

very exhausting to

comply with a demand!

All the people here on our planet are

offered help by Captain Calmer.

He teaches you how to stay

calm when you comply with a

demand.

I think I should now hand over to Captain Calmer...

"I have heard you have a helpful name for

demand avoidance on Earth, it is called

Pathological Demand Avoidance (PDA).

This is amazing as it means everyone

there is trying to understand why some

need to avoid demands to feel safe."

Well done, planet Earth! We here on planet Avoidance have been inspired by this. We now have a name for those who comply with demands, it is called Pathological Demand Compliance (PDC).

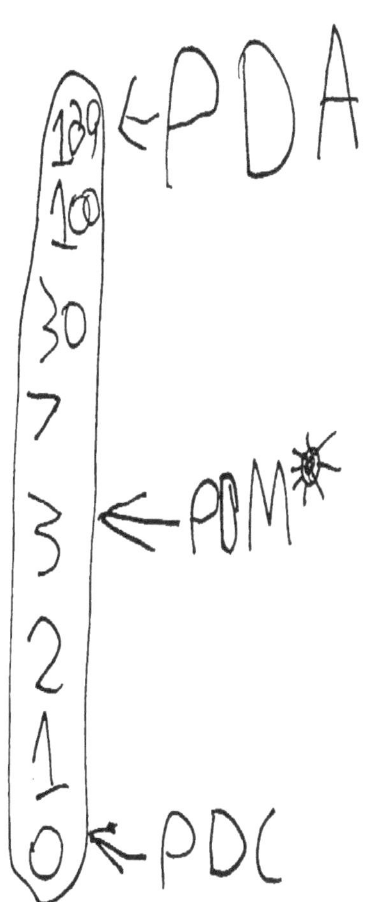

Why? So, we may understand the few on our planet who need support to feel safe by complying with demands.

*PATHOLOGICAL DEMAND MEDIUM

At one end we have those who have PDA, and must avoid demands.

Then in the middle people with PDM (Pathological Demand Medium). These people are in the middle of the scale and experience a mix of complying or avoiding demands.

At the opposite end of the scale is those with PDC (Pathological Demand Compliance). These people can comply to demands.

PDA/PDC Scale

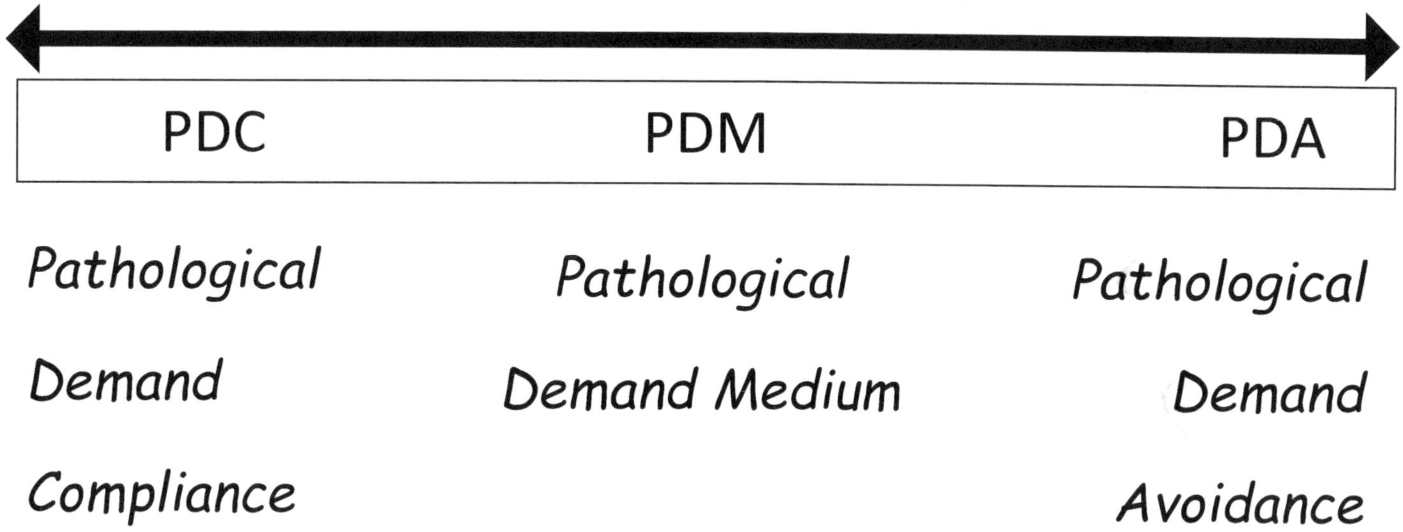

PDC	PDM	PDA

PDC	PDM	PDA
Pathological	*Pathological*	*Pathological*
Demand	*Demand Medium*	*Demand*
Compliance		*Avoidance*

(Most people on planet Earth are PDC but on planet Avoidance, we are mostly PDA people.)

Tools to support recovery with Captain Calmer...

Listening to music.   Reading a book.   Meditating.

Playing a game.   Cuddling a teddy.

Talking to someone.   Writing a story.   Watching a lava lamp.   Painting. Drawing. Lying down. Using a weighted blanket.   Playing with focus toys or Playdoh.

Blowing bubbles.

Wearing ear-defenders.   Playing with or cuddling a pet.

Tearing paper or popping bubble wrap.

"Anything can be a recovery tool... as long as it helps to calm you".

Questions:

What is Detective Demando's job?

What does the word crime mean on planet Avoidance?

What scares the people on planet Avoidance?

What demand did the teacher give to the boy in the story?

Where was the boy in the story taken to?

Who offers help to people on planet Avoidance?

On planet Avoidance, what name is given to those who comply with demands?

What did Captain Calmer and Detective Demando create?

What tools do you use to help you when you comply with a demand?

(Answers are on the last page!)

Word Search - PDA

```
C I Y L G U C I D H M E E G H N U
T A S T L R O E E I S N U L C E N
D T E L W O M I T I W H T H T A D
N E I D C I M D E M A N D S I T E
W W O H R S U E C N A D I O V A R
E G E C E I N S T R U C T I O N S
L I D R T C I H I H N G E R I P T
O L E T U I C A V H G W C H U H A
D C P I I E A T E N U R N O E B N
E O T O G L T C D N H A A A H I D
G H S E R T E H E I G T I S N D G
L T W S W D I S M S R O L E T G O
U G A H O H D T A C A O P E L I A
B N C A P T A I N C A L M E R H N
I H I I L S E E D N L D O T D B E
E I T N O R P P O A E C C C E O L
T B T F L G D P N P E R N G T S M
```

AVOIDANCE

CAPTAIN CALMER

COMMUNICATE

COMPLIANCE

CRIME

DEMANDS

DETECTIVE DEMANDO

INSTRUCTIONS

TOOL

UNDERSTAND

Pathological Demand Avoidance

Please be understanding,

when I scream and cry.

As sometimes I just do not know

why.

I want to do things,

I really do!

But not if there is a demand

from you.

Demands are not just from

you,

they seemingly come out of

the blue.

My body is in a struggle,

and my mind in a muddle.

The constant conflict within,

a meltdown about to begin.

Avoidance is the key,

to keep some sanity.

The world seems such a crazy place,

see the struggle upon my face.

My avoidance must be hasty,

to keep my safety!

I wrote this book to help children and adults to understand the anxiety behind PDA.

Demands increase anxiety and those with PDA must avoid any perceived demands. By doing so, they feel in 'control' and safe.

(Answers to questions.)

Detective Demando's job is to investigate avoidance and compliance crimes.

The word 'crime' means you have found a tool to cope with a demand and feel safe.

People on planet Avoidance are scared of demands.

The teacher told the boy to learn the alphabet, which is a demand.

The boy was taken to the Relaxation Jail as a reward so he could recover.

Captain Calmer offers help to those on planet Avoidance.

The name given to those who comply with demands and still feel safe, is Pathological Demand Compliance (PDC).

Captain Calmer and Detective Demando created a scale.

Lightning Source UK Ltd.
Milton Keynes UK
UKHW050906051022
409942UK00003B/192